For Fafa, Florian, and Sofia

First published in Great Britain in 1997 by Andersen Press Ltd.
First U.S. edition 1997

Library of Congress Cataloging-in-Publication Data
Testa, Fulvio.
A long trip to Z/written and illustrated by Fulvio Testa.
p. cm.
Summary: While flying around in an airplane, a child sees an alphabet of sights.
ISBN 0-15-201610-4
[1. Voyages and travels—Fiction. 2. Airplanes—Fiction. 3. Alphabet.] I. Title.
PZ7.T2875Lo 1997
[E]—dc21 96-47336

A C E F D B

Printed in Italy

Printed and bound in Italy by Grafiche AZ, Verona
Text and display type set in Bernhard Gothic

FULVIO TESTA

A LONG TRIP TO Z

HARCOURT BRACE & COMPANY

San Diego   New York   London

A is for **a**irplane. . . .

Climb inside and fly out of the **b**ook,

past the bird in its **c**age,

through the crack in the **d**oor.

"Good-bye, **e**lephant!
Good-bye, **f**ish!"

There is no time now to play your **g**uitar.

You fly up, up above the **h**ouse

and far away across a desert island.

Down below, a panther stretches in the **j**ungle.

You fly higher than the **k**ites.

You see someone fishing on a lake

and someone else climbing a **m**ountain.

You fly round and round the clock tower. It is **n**oon, and you still have far to go.

What can they see from the **o**bservatory?

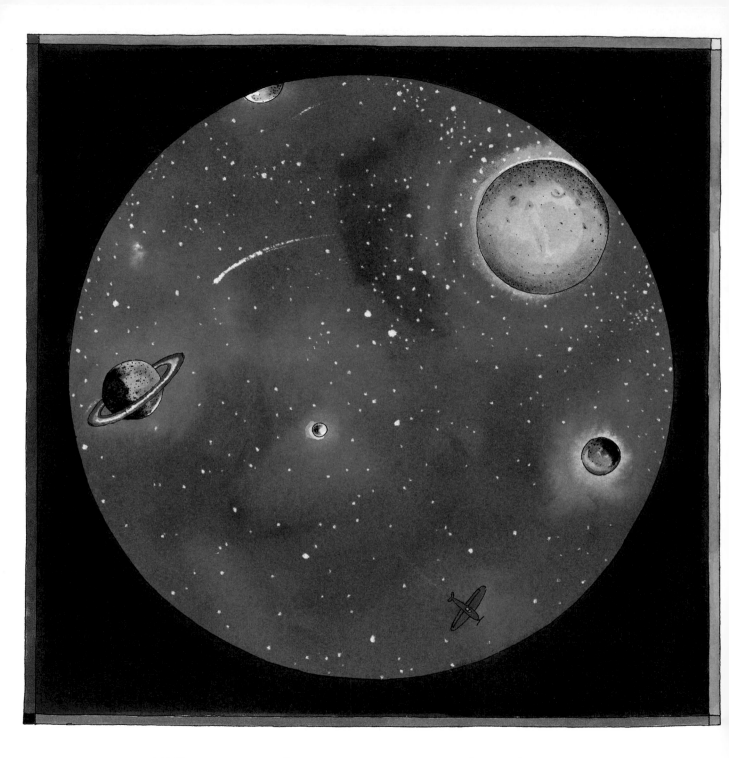

Why, you, of course, among the **p**lanets!

Time to go home! Fly in low over your warm **q**uilt,

and land safely near the **r**adio.

"Welcome back!" says Max, playing the **s**axophone.

Teddy waves his **t**ambourine.

"We missed you!" says Kittycat from behind the **u**mbrella.

"Yes, it's about time you came back to your book,"
grumbles Bunny, nibbling his **v**egetables.

Night has fallen. You see the moon through the **w**indow.

It is too late to play your **x**ylophone—
you are **y**awning.

Snuggle into your pillow with its pattern of galloping **z**ebras.
You've been on a long trip. Good night!